BIOLOGY
A Handbook of Skills for GCSE

Susan Tresman
B.Sc., Ph.D., P.G.C.E. (Cantab)

Nelson

Thomas Nelson and Sons Ltd
Nelson House   Mayfield Road
Walton-on-Thames   Surrey
KT12 5PL   UK

51 York Place
Edinburgh
EH1 3JD   UK

Thomas Nelson (Hong Kong) Ltd
Toppan Building 10/F
22A Westlands Road
Quarry Bay   Hong Kong

Distributed in Australia by

Thomas Nelson Australia
480 La Trobe Street
Melbourne   Victoria 3000
and in Sydney, Brisbane, Adelaide and Perth

© Susan Tresman 1987
First published by Thomas Nelson and Sons Ltd 1987
ISBN 0-17-448155-1
NPN 01

Printed in England
by Ebenezer Baylis & Son Ltd
The Trinity Press Worcester and London

All Rights Reserved. This publication is protected in the United Kingdom by the Copyright Act 1956 and in other countries by comparable legislation. No part of it may be reproduced or recorded by any means without the permission of the publisher. This prohibition extends (with certain very limited exceptions) to photocopying and similar processes, and written permission to make a copy or copies must therefore be obtained from the publisher in advance. It is advisable to consult the publisher if there is any doubt regarding the legality of any proposed copying.

Foreword

Not so long ago passing exams in biology meant learning and memorising a lot of facts. With the advent of GCSE things have changed. The emphasis now is not so much on recalling facts as on the development of skills. These include practical skills such as carrying out experiments, and theoretical skills involved in analysing and interpreting the results of experiments.

Dr. Tresman's book tells you which particular skills you need to acquire and how you can set about developing them. At first glance some of the skills may seem rather daunting, but if you persevere and master them they will stand you in good stead throughout your GCSE course.

Dr. Michael Roberts.

Acknowledgements

A number of people have helped in the production of *'Doing Biology'*. I would like to thank Mrs. Anne Shelton for critically reading an earlier draft of the manuscript and Geoffrey Tresman who typed the first version of the manuscript.
I owe particular thanks to Dr. Michael Roberts for his detailed constructive criticism of the manuscript and for the enthusiasm and encouragement he has shown throughout the project.
I would also like to thank my publishers, Thomas Nelson and Sons Ltd whose support is gratefully acknowledged.
I am grateful to the Midland Examining Group for their permission to reproduce specimen GCSE questions.
The woodlice experiment on page 4 is adapted from ABAL (1983) *Inquiry and Investigation in Biology: An Introduction*, Cambridge University Press.

Dr. Susan Tresman June 1987

Preface

In order to be successful at GCSE, pupils studying biology will be required to demonstrate their proficiency over a comprehensive range of practical and theoretical skills. These include: planning and writing reports of investigations; recording and organising results; performing calculations using a range of mathematical skills; writing succinctly on biological topics; planning projects; making notes and summaries; understanding new vocabulary and concepts.
Using numerous examples, *Doing Biology* describes how pupils can acquire and apply these skills.

Cover Photograph

Careful observation is an essential part of biology. Look closely at the front cover: it shows a duck's wing. Note the variety of colour. Can you see the different types of features? There are many differences in their size, shape and arrangement.
Look more closely and you may even see the fine features of individual barbs. Why does the water not soak into the features? Can you explain the advantage to the duck of any of the things you have seen? (*Ardea*)

CONTENTS

SECTION A

Doing Investigations in Biology

- Introduction — 2
- What is an investigation? — 2
- Planning an investigation — 7
- Writing down what you do — 7
- Writing a report of your investigation — 9
- Making biological drawings — 10
- Organising your results — 10
- Making your results easier to understand — 11
- Graphs — 12
- Frequency tables, histograms and bar charts — 16
- How accurate are your results? — 18
- It's easier to measure some things than others! — 18
- Hints on performing calculations — 20
- Organising other people's results: An example — 22
- Drawing conclusions — 27
- Linking practical experience with facts — 28

SECTION B

Developing the important study skills

- Introduction — 30
- Taking notes — 30
- Coping with new words — 31
- Scientific writing — 31
- Answering structured questions — 33
- Planning a project — 36
- Memorising and understanding things — 38
- How to make a good summary — 38
- Working with mathematics in biology — 39
- Checklist of skills for GCSE — 40
- Units of measurement — 42
- Index — 43

SECTION A
Doing Investigations in Biology

● **Introduction**

Biology is all about studying living things. A big part of studying biology is doing investigations. These are a good way of testing ideas and solving problems. When you are doing investigations you will usually be told what equipment to use and how to use it – but it will be up to you to get accurate results, write them down in your books, and make sense of them.
This section describes that you need to learn to help you make the most of the investigations you do in biology.

● **What is an investigation?**

Each time you do an investigation you will get involved in one or more of the following steps...

Making observations

This involves looking at things to help you to discover more about them. *Looking carefully* is very important; many of your investigations will be mostly doing just this. There are two types of observation.

a **Qualitative observations:** These describe a quality – something which you cannot measure. For example the colour, shape or taste of something.

b **Quantitative observations:** These describe a quantity – something which you can measure. For example length, volume, mass or time.

A set of observations is often called **data**.

Making a hypothesis

This involves suggesting an explanation for your observations.
Hypothesis is the word which describes a possible explanation for a set of observations. It may be only a 'hunch'.

Testing a hypothesis

You will need to test your hypothesis to find out if it is true. You can do this by –

either making your observations

or doing a practical investigation. This investigation should allow you to control conditions which you think will affect your hypothesis.

Interpreting your observations

By this stage you will have a set of observations. Some of these may be the results of an investigation. You need to look at these observations to see what they mean. This is called **interpreting your observations**.

Drawing a conclusion

You must try to decide if your interpretation of your observations supports your hypothesis? Has your hypothesis (your 'hunch') been shown to be true?
This is called **drawing a conclusion**.
You may have to look at the following example and see how the investigation follows the steps given above.
This way of doing an investigation is known as **the scientific method**. It can be summed up as follows:

> Making observations may lead on to making a hypothesis. The testing of a hypothesis involves more observations, or possibly a practical investigation. The final set of observations (including the results of any investigation) will need interpreting. This lead to the drawing of a conclusion – does your interpretation of your observations support your hypothesis?

If your observations do **not** support your hypothesis you may need to start again with *either* a new hypothesis *or* a different type practical investigation.

The Scientific Method

Making observations
↓
Making a hypothesis
↓
Testing a hypothesis
↓
Interpreting your observations
↓
↙ Drawing a conclusion ↘
Hypothesis supported   Hypothesis not supported:
by your observations   Make a new hypothesis
                        or try a different type
                        of investigation.

Example

Suppose you have set up a tank with some woodlice in it as shown in the diagram below. After two hours you have written down how many woodlice you found in each part of the tank.

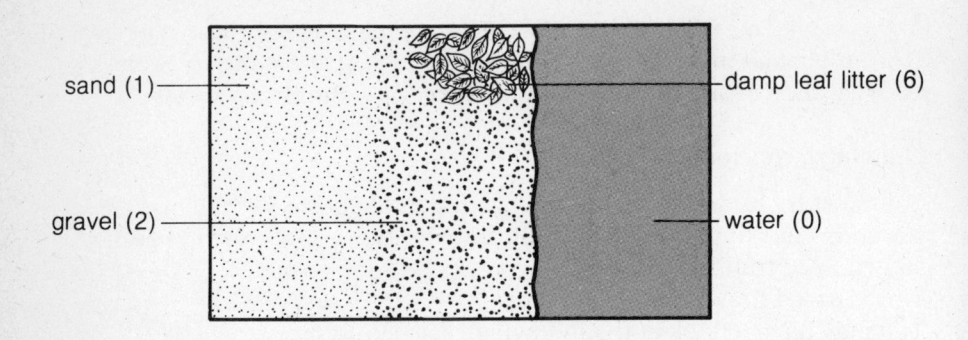

```
sand (1) ─────┐  ┌──────── damp leaf litter (6)
              │  │
gravel (2) ───┘  └──────── water (0)
```

What questions could you ask to help to explain what you found? Here are some examples:

Q. What **observations** have I made in this experiment?
A. There are six woodlice in the leaf-litter area, two in the gravel area, one in the sand area and none in the water area.

Q. What could have affected the distribution of woodlice?
A. *Amount of light* – do woodlice prefer darkness to light?
Humidity (or moisture) – do woodlice prefer damp or dry areas?
Amount of cover – do woodlice prefer to hide under leaf-litter rather than to be in the gravel or sand?
Amount of food – do woodlice feed on rotting leaves?

At this stage you do not know why the woodlice are found under the leaves. It could be because it is dark under there or because they like to be covered over by leaves rather than gravel or sand. They could be there because they are eating the leaves or because the leaves provide a damp covering. You have to make a sensible guess which fits in with the observations you've made on the woodlice in your tank – a **hypothesis**. For example:

Your hypothesis ... *'woodlice prefer damp environments'*.

You can **test your hypothesis** by doing some practical investigations.

To find out how woodlice react to humidity

1. Set up a choice chamber containing a dry area and a moist area as shown in the illustration below.

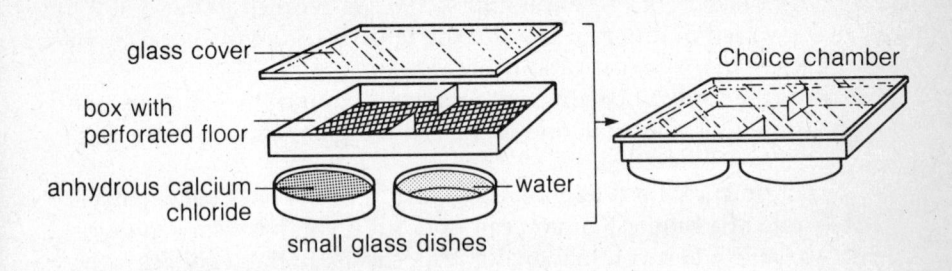

glass cover
box with perforated floor
anhydrous calcium chloride
water
small glass dishes
Choice chamber

Anhydrous calcium chloride powder absorbs water, so the air on this side of the choice chamber will become very dry. In contrast, the air above the water will become relatively humid. Wait at least ten minutes to allow time for these conditions to develop.

2. Place about ten woodlice in the choice chamber.
3. Observe the woodlice at intervals during the next half hour or so.

Which end of the choice chamber do woodlice seem to prefer?
Where do woodlice live, and how does this fit in with the results of your experiment?

When you have made all your observations, you will need to **interpret these observations** and **draw a conclusion**. You could then investigate other conditions which you may think will affect the woodlice. For example, how do woodlice react to light? How do they respond to different types of food or different surfaces (sand, gravel, etc)?

Variables

Conditions which can change (or *vary*) in a practical investigation are called **variables**. The idea of doing a practical investigation is to test your hypothesis by controlling the conditions of the investigation. This involves choosing one variable and deliberately allowing it to change. All the other variables must not be allowed to change – they must be kept constant.
If you change more than one variable at the same time you will not know how to explain the result. This is because you will not know *which* variable has caused the result.

Remember, the general rule is **change only one variable at a time**. You can see the sense of this if you look back to the woodlice example. The first set of observations did not allow you to decide if the distribution of woodlice depended on the amount of light, the humidity (or moisture), the amount of cover or presence of food. This is because *all* these conditions varied in different parts of the tank. So more than one variable was changing in the investigation.

Any one of them might be affecting where you found the woodlice. It is even possible that *more* than one of the changing variables are affecting the woodlice.

The idea of practical investigations is to test *all* of the possible variables **but only one at a time**. Then you can find out if you have chosen the correct variable when you made your hypothesis. In the woodlice investigation this would mean only allowing the *humidity* to change because the hypothesis was based on the *effect of* humidity.

Controls

Many of the practical investigations you do in biology will have a **control**. You need a control to give you a standard with which to compare the results of your investigation. The control experiment is exactly the same as your investigation but your chosen variable is *not* allowed to change. Look at this example to see how it works.

Suppose you want to test whether a pond snail gives off carbon dioxide when it breathes out. You will need to immerse the pond snail in something that indicates when carbon dioxide is being breathed in to it. This is called an *indicator*. Hydrogen carbonate indicator is red but turns yellow when carbon dioxide is present. You would set up two test tubes as shown in the diagram.

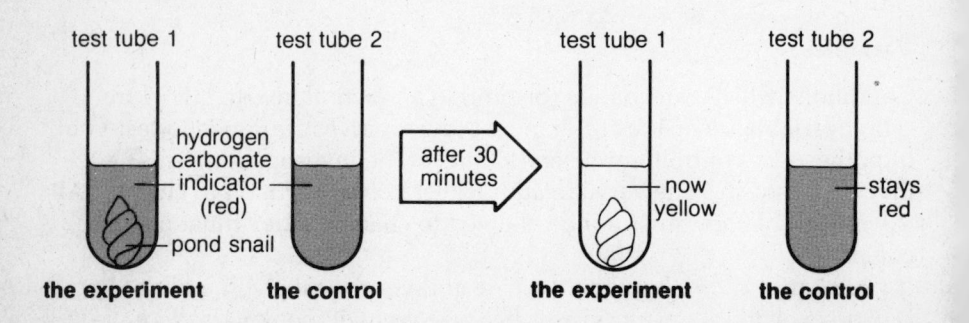

You can see that nothing has happened to the colour of the indicator in test tube **2** (the control). This shows that the colour change is **not** caused by the test tube, the liquid or the air.
The control *proves* that the pond snail must be causing the indicator to change in colour from red to yellow in test tube **1**. To *do* this the snail must be producing carbon dioxide.

- *Planning an investigation*

Usually you have to do an investigation in a limited amount of time. You are expected to get through a certain amount of work in the lesson, so you must try to do the best job you can in the time you have got.
This means that you have got to use your time wisely and **plan** what you are going to do.
You will usually be given instructions on how to do the investigation either on the blackboard or maybe as worksheets. The first thing to do is to **read** through the instructions to make sure that you know what you will be doing.
Sometimes there are parts of the investigation where you will be waiting for something to happen e.g. something to cool down or to heat up. Plan what you can be doing while you wait – maybe writing down what you have been doing in the investigation or some other details you need to help you understand the work you have to do in the lesson.
If you have only a limited amount of time don't forget to make lots of observations, so that your investigation makes sense when you look back on your notes. Write your observations down – nobody has a perfect memory!
Think **all the time** about what you are trying to find out by doing the investigation. Does what you are being asked to do make sense to you? When you think about the next step in the investigation, does it match up with the next instruction you have been given? If not, can you see why your ideas were different?

- *Writing down what you do*

One of the best ways of keeping a record of what you do is to use two books – one a lab notebook (or roughbook) and the other a main exercise book or folder.

Keeping a lab notebook

In this book, you should jot down **all** your comments, measurements, observations and calculations **while you are doing** the investigation. Remember to make a note of the *date* on which you do the work.
It is a good idea to write down your measurements in tables with a heading for each column and the units you are measuring in. Try to leave some space for corrections, for example:

Time (minutes)	Height of liquid in glass tube (cm)
0	0
10	2.1
20	4.3
30	5.9

Important points should be underlined so that they stand out.
If the experiment involves making calculations, **write down all your working** and not just the answer. Later on, you can't check on where you might have gone wrong if you've only got the final answer in your book.
If you write down a wrong number by mistake, don't write over it – there is always a danger of mis-reading the new number. Always cross out the wrong one and write the correct number next to it.
Do not be afraid to use plenty of space though you should avoid leaving big gaps. It is never a waste of paper to jot down notes about how the experiment is going, for example:

a   the reason why you decide to do some part of the experiment again, or repeat some reading;

b   you might think that some part of your experiment is not working properly – make a note of the problem;

c   any other checks you made during your experiment.

Sometimes your teacher may give you worksheets on which you just have to fill in some details about your investigation or measurements you have made.

Keeping a main exercise book/folder

You may have to transfer some, or all, of the reports you've made in your lab notebook into this book or folder. Your teacher will help you to decide exactly what to transfer. Some of your reports will need to go alongside theory work you do on the same topic. They may have to be written up fully into your main exercise book or folder or sometimes a cross reference to your lab notebook will be all that is needed. If you used a worksheet it may be sufficient to stick the completed worksheet into your main exercise book or folder.

- *Writing a report of your investigation*

You will usually be asked to write a report about your investigation, and this is a chance for you to sort out your ideas about *what* you have been doing and *why*. Often it is not until you have to write your ideas down that you sort them out properly in your mind.

In writing a report that makes sense of what you did in your investigation, it helps to follow a particular layout or format. Stick to that layout for all your reports if possible.

If you do not already follow a particular layout, try the following plan:

1 What did you try to find out by doing the investigation?
2 What equipment did you use to do it?
3 How did you set up the equipment (usually a diagram helps)?
4 What happened? What were your results and any other observations?
5 How successful were you in performing the investigation?

Try and always write down your report so that what you have found out would be clear to anyone else. *Why?* This is because someone may come along after you've done the experiment and want to:

a read all about it (they might be another student who missed that lesson);
b set up the investigation and repeat it;
c compare their results and practical methods with yours.

If you have drawn any graphs, then the results you used to draw them should also be included in your report – it helps you to make sense of your work.

If you made any special checks or took special care or found a part of your investigation difficult to do write this down in your report.

- **Making biological drawings**

By carefully doing drawing you can often explain things that would be difficult to describe in words. Even if you can do as good a job using words, it takes much longer than doing a drawing.

You don't need to be an artist to produce good biological drawings, provided you remember the following points.

1 Use a **pencil**.

2 Use a **sharp** pencil – preferably HB in strength. Don't press too hard on the page or it will be difficult to make any neat, clear corrections.

3 Make your drawings **large enough** to be clear – up to half a page in size and well spaced out.

4 **Label** your drawings, making sure that you include all the important names of things you have drawn. Use a ruler to draw the line from the label to the point on the drawing you are labelling – make sure your line goes **exactly** to this point. Use a pen to write the labels.

5 Give your drawing a **title**, so that you know what it is and the person reading your work knows what it is. Don't forget to underline the title.

6 Don't use colour unless you are told to.

7 Sometimes you may need to add a **scale** to your drawing. A good way of doing this is to use the scale factor. This is written alongside the drawing – '$\times 2$' means that every measurement of the drawing is twice the size of the real object; '$\times \frac{1}{2}$' means half the size of the real object.

Don't forget to refer to your drawing in the written part of your report. It is tempting to treat the written part and the diagram(s) separately but remember the diagram is an important part of the whole report and links in very closely with what you have written.

- *Organising your own results*

Through your practical work in biology you will collect results. These could be measurements, temperature readings, or numbers of organisms. In order to make sense of your results you have first to **organise** them and then to **analyse** them.

When you are doing an investigation it is worth thinking about how you are going to record your results **before** you start to collect them. This helps you to sort out **what kind of observations and measurements** you will write down. It also helps you to get them down efficiently and accurately.

This type of table is a good way of recording numbers of things:

Comparison of where two types of plant are found (A & B)

	Number in open grass		Number in shaded woodlands		
	Score	Number	Score	Number	Total
Plant A	ⅢⅢ III	8	ⅢⅡ	5	13
Plant B	0	0	ⅢⅡ ⅢⅡ	10	10
		8		15	23

Remember these rules when you are writing out **tables**:

1 Always give the table a **heading**.

2 Do not include too many results in one table, it only gets confusing.

3 Record the numbers counted as a score as shown in the example above. Note that a score of '5' is recorded as ⅢⅡ

4 Always set out your tables very **clearly** and use plenty of **space**. This allows room for any corrections.

5 Do not leave blanks in the tables. A zero value should be shown as a 0 and a missing observation as a dash –).

6 When giving measurements use the correct standard units (usually SI units as shown on page 42).

7 Always include the actual number of things you counted or measured in your first table. To prevent the table becoming too crowded you can always use a second table to sort out or analyse your results.

● *Making your results easier to understand*

After you have written down what has happened in your investigation you will need to make sense of what you have seen. Presenting or showing your results (or data) as **percentages, frequency tables** or **graphs** will often help you to do this.

If you have gathered lots of results, then you may find it helps to work out certain values that summarise all your results. This may help to tell you something about your results. You can see how to work out these types of values in the section called 'Hints on performing calculations' on page 20.

Percentages

If you need to change your results to percentages, remember to record these in a second table. Always say where the original results are – they will usually be in either your lab notebook or your exercise book. Here is an example of how you could do this.
The results recorded in the table on page 11 have been changed to percentages in the table below.

Comparison of where two types of plant (A & B) are found shown as percentages

	Percentage in open grass	Percentage in shaded woodlands	Total
Plant A	62%	38%	100%
Plant B	0	100%	100%

If you don't know how to work out percentages (or if you forgotten what to do), this example has been worked out for you in the section 'Hints on performing calculations' on page 21.

● *Graphs*

Why use graphs?

It is not often easy to see patterns just by looking at some tables of results which you might get from your experiments. This is when it is a good idea to draw a **graph**. Graphs can help you to sort out data if they are drawn out carefully and accurately.

The type of graph you should draw for a particular experiment depends on the type of data you have collected.
You should draw a **line graph** for a set of *single* or *'isolated' results* and a **bar chart** or a **histogram** for a set of results that are *grouped* in some way. The examples below will give you more idea about these general points.

Line graphs

Here are a few rules for making good line graphs:

1. Use a **sharp pencil** to draw lines and points as neatly as possible.
2. Give the graph a **title** saying what it is meant to show.
3. The *axes* of the graph are shown below; they are two straight lines – the **x** axis goes **across** and the **y** axis goes **up**. It is important to know which is which! Remember X = 'a cross'.

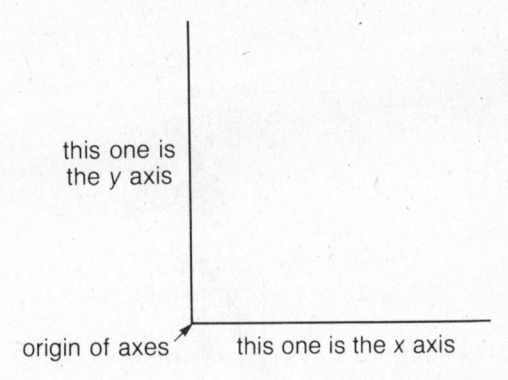

this one is the y axis

origin of axes   this one is the x axis

4. The *origin* of the graph is the point where the two axes meet. Usually this point has the value x = 0, y = 0 i.e. (0, 0). The numbers increase up the y axis and to the right along the x axis.
5. *Sometimes* you can get a better idea of the pattern between the two variables you are investigating if you do not have the origin at (0, 0). Look at these two graphs.

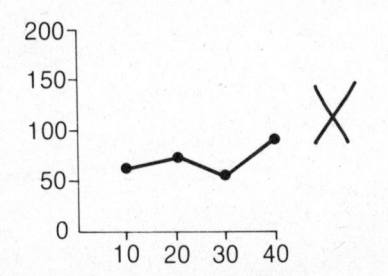

Can you see what is wrong with the graph? The points are all crowded together in the middle part of the graph, and most of the graph is empty. This makes it a lot more difficult to work out any pattern.

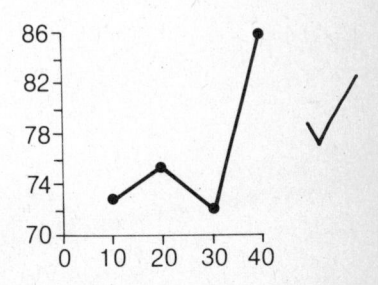

This is a much better use of the space. The y axis is now more closely matched to the points. You can get a much more detailed idea of the pattern of the graph.

6   Take care in choosing your scales so that the points you plot take up most of the length of the axes: you should aim for a graph like that on the left.

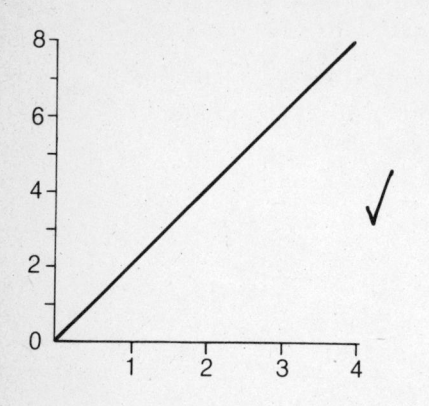

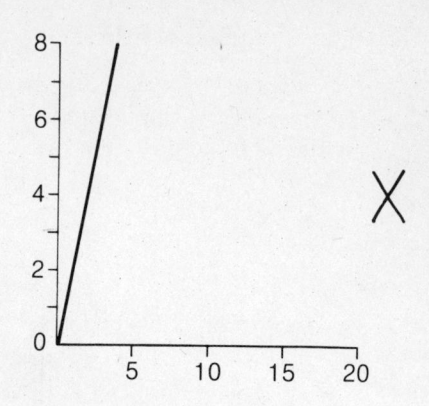

7   Label both axes fully and give the units (if relevant):
    e.g.   masses of things in *grams* (g);
           heights of things in *centimetres* (cm) or *metres* (m);
           time in *seconds* (s);
           temperature in *degrees Celsius* (°C).

8   It is important to be able to **fit a line to the points**. You do this by trying to join up all the points, like the example below. Another advantage of this type of graph is that it makes it easy to estimate values *between* points you have measured. For example:

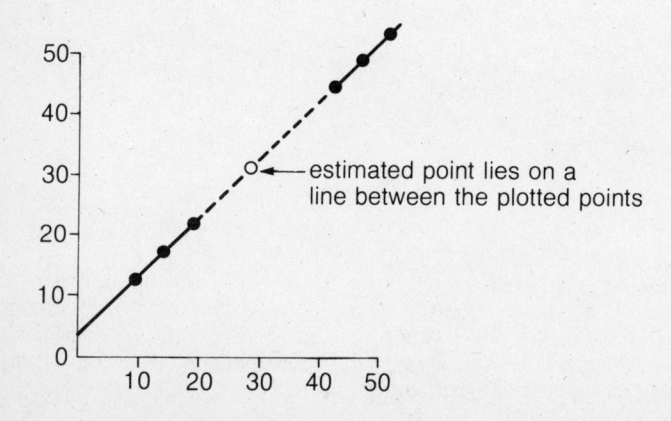

estimated point lies on a line between the plotted points

9   When you draw the graph, you may see that one of the results seems way 'off-course' from the other values. Try and check this one again, because it may be wrong. Do *not* leave it out, you should always include *all* your results. If you can't check it again, then its worth saying that you are not sure about that particular result.

10 Sometimes you may need to put two or more sets of results on the same graph – so you need a way of telling between them.

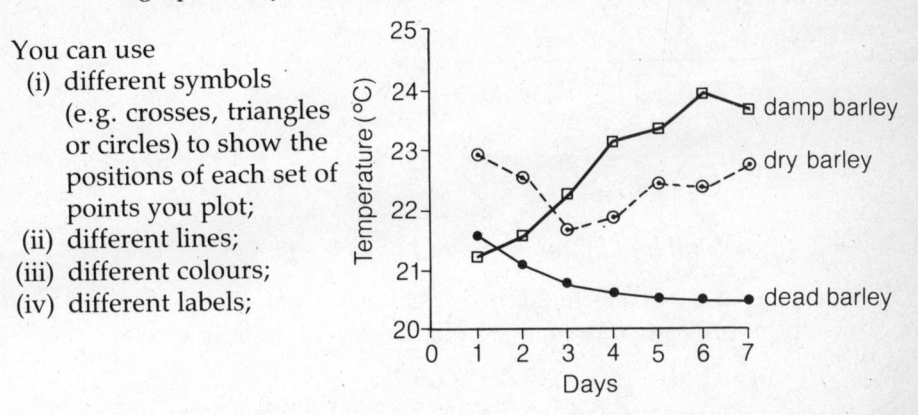

You can use
 (i) different symbols (e.g. crosses, triangles or circles) to show the positions of each set of points you plot;
 (ii) different lines;
 (iii) different colours;
 (iv) different labels;

Here is an example of a line graph that puts all of these rules together. The results used to draw the graph are shown overleaf.

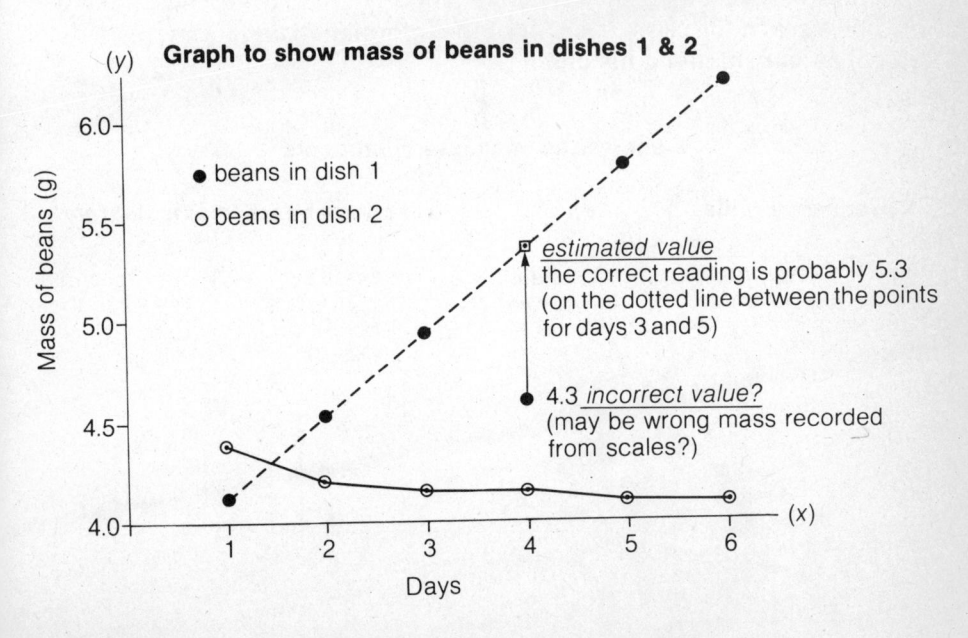

Graph to show mass of beans in dishes 1 & 2

- beans in dish 1
- ○ beans in dish 2

estimated value
the correct reading is probably 5.3 (on the dotted line between the points for days 3 and 5)

4.3 *incorrect value?*
(may be wrong mass recorded from scales?)

The table shows the mass of the dishes of beans, where **Dish 1** was watered regularly, while **Dish 2** was not watered (see the graph on page 15).

Day	1	2	3	4	5	6
Dish of beans 1 mass (g)	4.10	4.35	4.90	4.30	5.75	6.20
Dish of beans 2 mass (g)	4.30	4.20	4.15	4.15	4.10	4.10

● *Frequency tables, histograms and bar charts*

Certain types of data collected in investigations is not so easy to understand if presented as a line graph. Look at the example below.

Shoe sizes in a class: 6,6,5,6,2,7,4,6,3,4,5,7,9,8,6,5,10,7 6,6,5,4,7,6,5,8,3,4,5,6,7,8,3,4,5,7

This information can be organised into a **frequency table**. The frequency table for these results is shown below. This gives an idea of the variation in shoe sizes in the class. It sorts out the information and it can be used to prepare a **bar chart** or a **histogram**.

Shoe sizes in a class of students

Frequency table

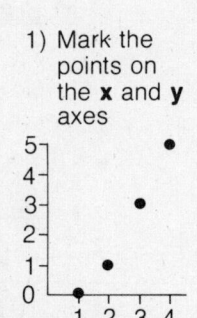

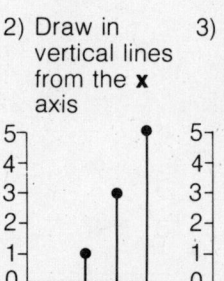

Shoe size	Number of students
1	0
2	1
3	3
4	5
5	7
6	9
7	6
8	3
9	1
10	1
11	0

Preparing a bar chart or histogram

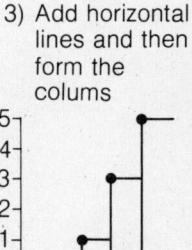

1) Mark the points on the **x** and **y** axes

2) Draw in vertical lines from the **x** axis

3) Add horizontal lines and then form the colums

Completed histogram

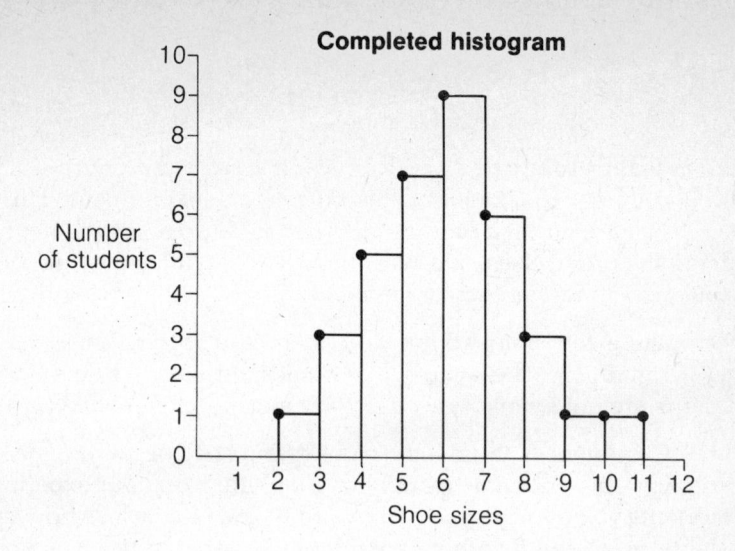

[Histogram: Number of students vs Shoe sizes. Values: size 2:1, size 3:3, size 4:5, size 5:7, size 6:9, size 7:6, size 8:3, size 9:1, size 10:1, size 11:1]

The kind of bar chart shown is called a histogram. In a **histogram** the variable on the **x** axis is shown as a sequence of numbers. This means that the area of each column is proportional to the frequency of that value. Most of the rules for line graphs apply to histograms but remembers the two extra given below.

a The values for the variable being observed are put along the **x** axis (in this case, shoe size). The frequency of the variable goes up the **y** axis (in this case, 'how many people take each shoe size?').

b Make the columns the same width.

Bar charts

Bar charts are quite like histograms but there are often gaps between the bars because the variable being looked at along the x axis is not a sequence of numbers – it is more of a 'label' than a measurement.

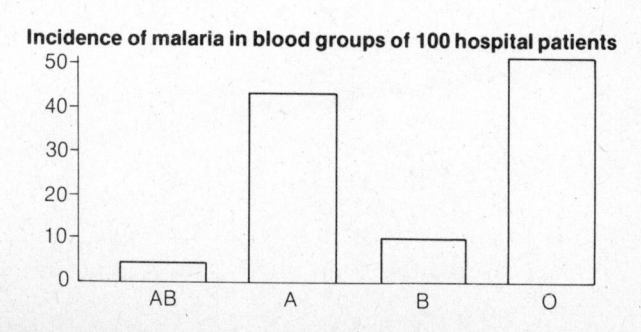

Incidence of malaria in blood groups of 100 hospital patients

[Bar chart: AB ≈ 4, A ≈ 43, B ≈ 9, O ≈ 50]

17

- ## How accurate are your results?

You will be trying to get reliable results but here are some of the ways that the reliability of your results can be affected.

1 Human Error: Take care to read scales, masses etc. very carefully, *especially* if you have to take lots of readings in one experiment. This often crops up if you are doing a class experiment – your results will never be the same as everyone elses, because other people will be making their own small errors in what they are doing.

2 Instrument error: Some of the equipment you will be using will have their own limitations. Its easy to see examples of this e.g. rulers where the divisions are not evenly spaced, a slow stopwatch and so on.

3 'Outside' influences: Sometimes an experiment goes wrong because something you have not anticipated has a big effect on your experiment and the results you get. Suppose you were trying to measure how quickly a plant takes up water; just think what would happen if the twig you have cut is frozen because of the low temperature outside!

4 Unrepresentative results: It is always a good idea to **take more than one reading** of something if you can. This gives you an idea of how consistent the feature is that you are measuring. The best way to cut down on the variation between results and to increase your confidence in your results is to increase the number (or sample) of results you have got. Either you have got to do more than one, or you can compare your results with those of other students.

- ## Its easier to measure some things than others!

Here's an example to show you why!

Measure the diameter of these two circles.

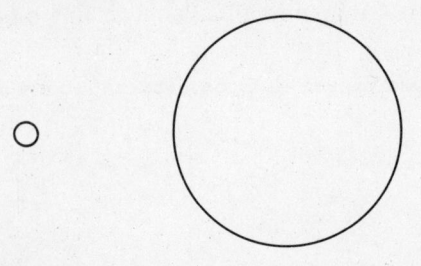

If all your friends measured the same circle you would not get the same answers.

Which circle can you measure more accurately? It is the biggest circle. There are problems of how accurately you use your ruler to measure but the *bigger* something is the *less* important is the error. A slight error in the measurement of the smaller circle will have a larger effect on the result than a slight error in the measurement of the larger circle. You can see how this happens by looking at the example below. If you are not sure how to work out averages, then look at page 20 before you read on.

Measurements by pupils:

Large Circle (mm)	Small Circle (mm)
31.0	4.0
29.5	2.5
28.5	3.5
32.5	3.0
31.0	2.5
30.5	2.0
30.0	2.0
32.5	—
28.5	
29.0	
27.0	
33.0	

Average 30 mm (±3 mm)
i.e. biggest 33 mm; smallest 27 mm

$$\text{Average} = \frac{21.5 \text{ mm}}{7} = 3 \text{ mm } (\pm 1 \text{ mm})$$

i.e. biggest 4.0 mm; smallest 2.0 mm

$$\frac{1}{3} \times 100 = \textbf{33\% error}$$

$$\frac{3}{30} \times 100 = \textbf{10\% error}$$

You can see the error as a percentage of the average in both cases. The **largest error** (33%) is in the measurement of the **smaller** circle.

General error calculation

$$\frac{1}{2}\Big[(\text{highest value}) - (\text{lowest value})\Big] = \text{limit of error}$$

Percentage error calculation

$$\frac{\text{limit of error}}{\text{average measurement}} \times 100 = \text{percentage error}$$

• Hints on performing calculations

Ranges

This is difference from the biggest value to the smallest value.

	Shoe sizes	Number of people taking that size
	1	0
	2	1
	3	3
	4	5
	5	7
Range	6	9 **The mode**
	7	6
	8	3
	9	1
	10	1
	11	0

The **range** in this example is from size 2 to size 10

Averages

1 The mean: To calculate the mean you **add all the values** you have got and **divide** the total by the **number of values** you have just added up – like this:

Value	1	2	3	4	5	Total of 5 values
Measurement	6.0 cm	5.5 cm	6.2 cm	5.7 cm	6.1 cm	= 29.5 cm

$$\frac{29.5 \text{ cm}}{5} = 5.9 \text{ cm} = \frac{\text{Mean average}}{\text{measurement}} = \frac{\text{Total of all values}}{\text{Total number of values}}$$

2 The mode: This the **most common** value. In this case it is the shoe size that **most** people take – so the mode is size 6. If you draw a **histogram** for these results, the mode is the shoe size with the **tallest** column (see page 17).

3   **The median:** If all the separate values are arranged in a list of ascending order, the median value is the one which is in the middle of the list.

Working out percentages

A percentage value gives the value as a fraction out of a total of one hundred. This example shows how to work out the percentages given on page 11:

Plant A
Total number of plants = 13 = **100%** of your sample **of plant A**.
Number in open grass = 8
To find what percentage this figure is of the total you divide 8 by the total and then multiply by 100:

$$\frac{8}{13} \times 100 = 61.53\%$$

This is then rounded up to 62% because it is above half-way between 61% and 62%.

Number in shaded woodlands = 5

$$\frac{5}{13} = 100 = 38.46\% \text{ (rounded down to 38\%)}$$

As **all** the plant **A** grows in *either* open grass *or* shaded woodland, adding these two percentages together will give 100%: 62% + 38% = 100%

Plant B
Total number of plants = 10 = **100%** of your sample **of plant B**.
Number in open grass = 0
So 0% of plant **B** grow in open grass
All the plant **B** (10) grows in shady woodlands, so we can say 100% of them grow in shady woodland.

Working out percentage increase

If you are taking a series of measurements of something you may need to work out by how much it has increased since the first measurement. You can do this by working out the **percentage increase** between the two measurements. Look at the example overleaf.

Suppose you want to find out by how much your pet hamster will increase in size during the first three months that you own it. You can do this by measuring the hamster's length once a week. It is best to measure its length on the same day each week. Then you can work out the percentage increase in size which occurs between your first and last readings, three months apart.

$$\text{Percentage increase in length of hamster after three months} = \frac{\left(\begin{array}{c}\text{length of hamster}\\\text{at the end}\\\text{of three months}\end{array}\right) - \left(\begin{array}{c}\text{length of hamster}\\\text{when you first}\\\text{measured it}\end{array}\right)}{(\text{length of hamster when you first measured it.})} \times 100$$

Suppose the measurements are 50 cm at the start and 75 cm after three months:

$$\text{Percentage increase} = \frac{(75 \text{ cm}) - (50 \text{ cm})}{50 \text{ cm}} \times 100$$

$$= \frac{25 \text{ cm}}{50 \text{ cm}} = 0.5 \times 100 = 50\%$$

The percentage sign (%) is always added to show that the figure is a percentage value. The percentage increase in size is 50%; an increase of 50% tells you that it has grown by half its original length.

General method of calculating percentage increase:

$$\frac{(\text{last measurement}) - (\text{first measurement})}{(\text{first measurement})} \times 100 = \text{percentage increase}$$

- *Organising other peoples results: An example*

Sometimes you will be given sets of results to interpret from investigations that other people have done – you need to be able to organise the results.
Suppose you were given the following data:

Numbers of flowers on foxglove plants
The table below represents the number of flowers on the stems of foxgloves at two different sites (**A** and **B**). This table is called an array. An **array** is the original set of figures which you record i.e. *before* you reorganise the results into a more convenient order. Is there any noticeable difference in the number of flowers per stem amongst the foxgloves found at the two sites?

	Site **A**: sunny bank	Site **B**: shady, moist woodland
Number of flowers on the stems of foxgloves	7 12 9 5 9 7 10 6 7 8 3 7 11 4 15 8 11 9 7 6 9 5 6	3 6 11 7 4 3 6 2 5 2 2 4 3 5 5 3 8 4 3 1 3 2 5

You could organise the results by following the five steps given below.

1 Drawing up **frequency tables** for the sunny and shady sites (**A** and **B**).

2 Drawing **histograms** of the results in the frequency table for sites **A** and **B**.

3 Calculating the **range**, the **mean**, the **median** and the **mode** for the foxglove stems observed at these two sites. See pages 20 and 21 for details of the calculations.

4 **Describing the differences** between the two sites by considering the range, mean, median and mode values.

5 **Drawing your conclusions** from these results.

These steps have been worked out for you here. You can refer back to this example when you have to organise a set of results.

Drawing up frequency tables

Organise the original set of figures (the array) into frequency tables for the sunny and shady sites (**A** and **B**).

Site **A**: sunny bank		Site **B**: shady woodland	
Number of flowers on stems	Foxgloves of this type	Number of flowers on stems	Foxgloves of this type
3	1	1	1
4	1	2	4
5	2	3	6
6	3	4	3
7	5	5	4
8	2	6	2
9	4	7	1
10	1	8	1
11	2	9	0
12	1	10	0
13	0	11	1
14	0	Total number in sample	23*
15	1		
Total number in sample	23*		

(*see overleaf)

* Make sure that the total in the frequency table is equal to the total number of figures in the original set (the array). It is easy to miss out a figure as you transfer them into the frequency table. A good way of preventing this is to *cross off* values as you put them in the frequency table. For example:
If you want to transfer the details of those foxgloves with five flowers at site **A** from array A into the frequency table, try to do it like this. Search down or across each row, *one at a time*, checking for the value you need. There is less chance of missing one if you do it this way.

Site **A**: sunny bank
```
 7  12  9  5̷  9  7  10  6
 7   8  3̷  7  11  4̷ 15  8
11   9  7  6   9  5̷  6
```

There is a total of 23 values in the array

You have already crossed out the details of foxgloves with only three and four flowers (one of each). Now you find that there are only two foxgloves with five flowers each. Carry on doing this until all the numbers in the array are crossed through. That way you won't miss any of the 23 values. It is a good idea to use a pencil to cross through the numbers in the array. That way you can still read the numbers in case you need to check them again.

Drawing histograms from frequency tables

Represent the contents of the frequency tables as two histograms as shown opposite. Look back to page 16 for details of how to draw a histogram.

Look back at the frequency tables for sites **A** and **B** on page 23. Often only one or two foxgloves show a particular number of flowers on their stems. Sometimes if you have several low values it is best to reorganise them into a grouped frequency table. A **grouped frequency table** combines into groups the separate values from the original frequency table. (These groups are normally of equal size.)

In the grouped frequency table opposite, the groups cover three possible numbers of flowers on a stem: (1,2,3), (4,5,6), (7,8,9), (10,11,12), (13,14,15). The number of foxgloves which fit into each group is found by adding up the relevant values in the original frequency table. For example, *one* foxglove has four flowers, *two* have five flowers and *three* have six flowers – so there are *six* foxgloves which have either four, five or six flowers.

Numbers of flowers on foxglove stems
Site **A**: sunny bank

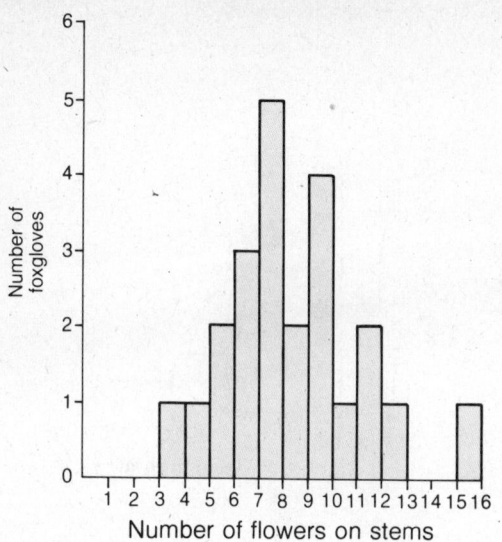

Number of flowers on foxglove stems
Site **B**: shady woodland

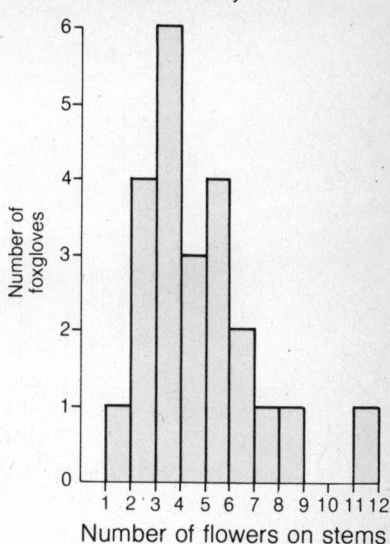

Examples of grouped frequency tables:

Site **A**: sunny bank

Number of flowers on stems	Number of foxgloves of this type
1–3	1
4–6	6
7–9	11
10–12	4
13–15	1
Total number in sample	23

Site **B**: shady woodland

Number of flowers on stems	Number of foxgloves of this type
1–3	11
4–6	9
7–9	2
10–12	1
13–15	0
Total number in sample	23

The histograms for grouped frequency tables are prepared in much the same way as before.

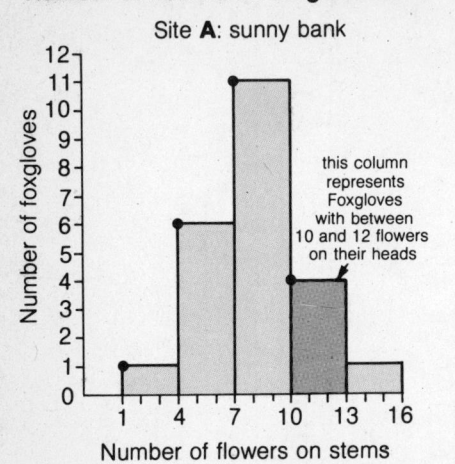

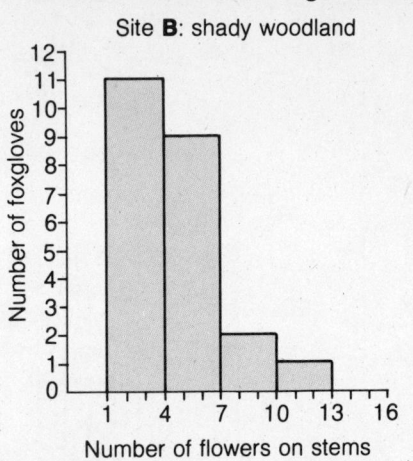

Number of flowers on foxglove stems
Site **A**: sunny bank

this column represents Foxgloves with between 10 and 12 flowers on their heads

Number of flowers on foxglove stems
Site **B**: shady woodland

Calculating the range, mean, median and mode

Range   Site **A**: 3–15 flowers on a stem
            Site **B**: 1–11 flowers on a stem

Mean

	Total number of flowers	Total number of stems	Mean average
Site A	194	23	194/23 = 8.4 flowers on a stem
Site B	103	23	103/23 = 4.5 flowers on a stem

Median

	Total number of values	Lower 'half' of values	Middle value	Upper half of values	Median value
Site A	23	7 or less	7	8 or more	7 flowers on a stem
Site B	23	3 or less	4	4 or more	4 flowers on a stem

Mode   Most frequent value – Site **A**: 7 flowers on a stem
                                 Site **B**: 3 flowers on a stem

Summary

	Flowers on a stem			
	Range	Mean	Median	Mode
Site **A**	3–15	8.4	7	7
Site **B**	1–11	4.5	4	3

For further details of these calculations, see pages 20 and 21.

Describing the differences

There is a wider range in the numbers of flowers on a stem at site **A** than there is at site **B**. The range at site **A** is also includes higher numbers of flowers on a stem.
Site **A** has nearly twice the mean number of flowers on a stem compared to site **B**.
Almost half the foxgloves at site **A** eight or more flowers on their stems. However, nearly half the foxgloves at site **B** have only three flowers or less on their stems.
The most common number of flowers on a stem at site **A** is seven to a stem. At site **B** the most common number is only three flowers to a stem.

Drawing a conclusion

Foxgloves that grow on sunny sites generally form twice as many flowers on their stems as those foxgloves that grow on shady sites.

• *Drawing conclusions*

You will usually be asked to **explain** any results you get from your investigations – why did what you saw actually happen? If the investigation is about something completely new to you, then it is not easy to do this. These are the steps you should take to help you work out what happened in your investigation. This is called **drawing a conclusion**.

1. Get as full a set of results as you can. You might need to check your results with other people in the class to make sure they are sensible.

2. Decide how best to organise your results so that they are easy to understand. You can use some of the methods that have already been explained to you.

3   Look for **patterns** in each set of results. Also look for patterns **between** different sets of results if you've had more than one go at the investigation (or if you've tested more than one set of variables in the same investigation).

4   Do these results look similar to anything you've come across before? For example, if you are testing the effect of temperature on something, have you seen temperature have a similar effect in a previous investigation?

5   Can you use the facts you have been given in your other lessons to help you explain what you have seen?

6   Would it help to do some extra reading on the subject, or a similar subject? Look in your text book or the library.

7   If you can't make any headway with any of the above ideas, ask your teacher for some help.

Once you have worked out the conclusions, make a note in your laboratory notebook of any other investigations you have done that showed a similar result. This helps to build up links between certain areas of the syllabus. It can also illustrate important biological principles.

● *Linking practical experience with facts*

It is easy to get into the habit of seeing theory and practical as two separate halves of biology. What can you do to help to build a bridge between the two?
Here are some ideas – find out which work best for you and get into the habit of doing them regularly.

1   Each time you do an investigation, check over what you have been doing in your last few theory lessons. The two will usually be related to each other. You might want to introduce your investigation with a brief summary of any relevant theory notes. This can help to set the scene for the investigation.

2   Operate a cross-reference system between your laboratory notebook and theory exercise book and also any relevant pages in your textbook. This will make it easier for you to flick from related ideas in your theory and practical lessons. A date or page number or investigation number may be enough to help you.

3   Sometimes you don't have time to discuss what has gone on in your investigation at the end of the practical lesson. Try your own 'follow-

up session' as soon after the practical lesson as you can. Try to interpret your results and see how they are related to any background theory you have learned recently (it need only take ten minutes or so of your time).

4   If you have discovered new ideas as a result of an investigation, write about them **in your own words** while they are *fresh in your mind*. Sort them out as far as you can and try to understand how they can be fitted into your own knowledge of biology.

SECTION B
Developing the Important Study Skills

● **Introduction**

In addition to practical biology, the other main part of your course is theoretical biology. If you want to get the most out of your theory lessons, then you need to develop certain skills that will help you to be successful. This section of the book explains how to go about developing them.

● **Taking notes**

Sometimes your teacher may give you notes. Other times you will have to make your **own** notes.

What is the point of notes?

In some lessons you will study some aspects of biology in different ways – talks by the teacher, films and videos, class discussions or simply by reading books. In time, you may forget the information learned through these methods. To avoid this problem you should make your own notes of these lessons. Often you only need to write down the most important points and this can be done very quickly.

How to make good notes

1. Make your notes **short** and **clear** so that you can read through them quickly and easily. Just writing down some information will help you to remember it.

2. Include all the main ideas as headings and underline them, and then group relevant points under each heading.

3. If you are making notes from a textbook, it is often a good idea to reorganise and reword what it says in the text book. This means you can put the information in a form that is more useful to you. Your notes should be your **own summary** of what the text book is saying. This could involve linking the new information to other things you have been learning about or adding your own comments or making cross references to other parts of your exercise book.

4   Remember, you have got to make any new information really *mean* something to you. **Make sure you understand what you write down**. If you don't understand it when you write it down, you will have no chance of understanding it later!

● Coping with new words

You will be expected to understand the meaning of many specialised biological words as you go through your course. To help you remember them, try the following idea:
Get a separate exercise book and when you start a new topic put the new topic as a heading at the top of a new page. Leave a large margin and write down all the key words when you meet them for the first time. Don't forget to write down what they mean! As you learn more about a topic, you will begin to realise that groups of new words all link together. You can show this by using arrows or a colour coded system or another system that works well for you. An example is shown overleaf.

● Scientific writing

You will often be asked to write down what you know about a subject or to write a short explanation about something. Here are three examples of questions you might come across:
Give a biological *explanation* for each of the following:

a   Green plants are energy converters and food producers in food chains.
b   Yeast is used in both the baking and the brewing industries.
c   Conservationists are concerned with keeping hedgerows.

To answer these questions successfully –

1   Make sure you are quite clear what you are being asked to write about. **Slowly read through the question** (or each part of the question). **Read it at least twice** to make sure that you understand it.

2   Jot down the most important points in a short **list** before you answer the question.

3   **Check your list** to make sure that you have included all the most important points. Often the answer will have to be less than four lines and still cover all the main points.

4   Use as few words as possible to make your point. **Keep it simple**, use short sentences, then your answer will be clear and easy to follow. There's no point using long words and sentences if you don't need to.

- **An example of how to cope with new words:**

BREATHING SYSTEMS IN MAN

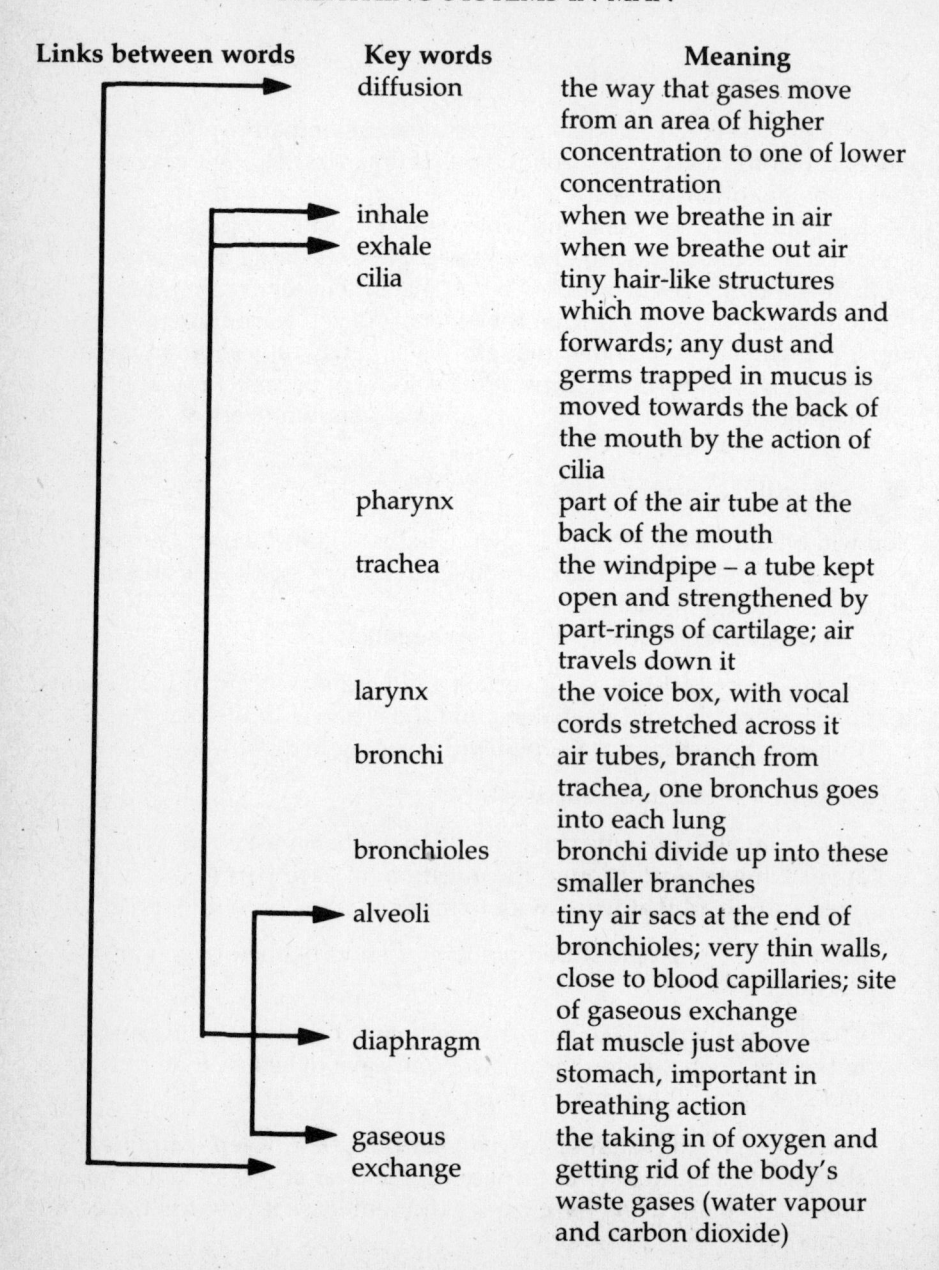

Links between words	Key words	Meaning
	diffusion	the way that gases move from an area of higher concentration to one of lower concentration
	inhale	when we breathe in air
	exhale	when we breathe out air
	cilia	tiny hair-like structures which move backwards and forwards; any dust and germs trapped in mucus is moved towards the back of the mouth by the action of cilia
	pharynx	part of the air tube at the back of the mouth
	trachea	the windpipe – a tube kept open and strengthened by part-rings of cartilage; air travels down it
	larynx	the voice box, with vocal cords stretched across it
	bronchi	air tubes, branch from trachea, one bronchus goes into each lung
	bronchioles	bronchi divide up into these smaller branches
	alveoli	tiny air sacs at the end of bronchioles; very thin walls, close to blood capillaries; site of gaseous exchange
	diaphragm	flat muscle just above stomach, important in breathing action
	gaseous exchange	the taking in of oxygen and getting rid of the body's waste gases (water vapour and carbon dioxide)

● *Answering structured questions*

Although a structured question is usually about one topic, it is split up into lots of different parts. Each part may ask you about a different aspect of the overall topic. Sometimes you will be asked to work out a calculation or to draw a graph or fill in numbers in a table. You might be given some results and asked to suggest a reason for any pattern the results show. You will need to use a mixture of skills to answer different parts of these questions. Suppose you were given this question after studying the subject of photosynthesis:

Question
Figure 1 below shows part of a vertical section through a green leaf.

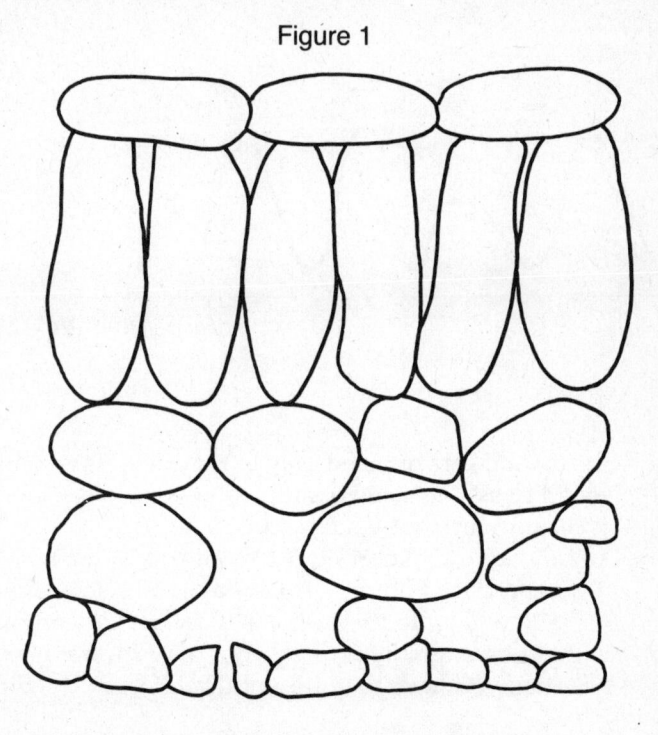

Figure 1

a On Figure 1 above,
  (i) label a guard cell and a palisade mesophyll cell,
  (ii) draw a small circle in each of the cells that contain chloroplasts.

b As a result of photosynthesis, plants make sugar. State one use of this sugar to
  (i) the plant itself,
  (ii) humans

c The graph, in Figure 2 below, shows how much sugar is being produced by a green plant over a period of several days, under natural conditions.
   (i) Suggest one reason why less sugar was produced during day 2.
   (ii) Draw a line on the graph to show how much sugar would be produced if the plant was kept under continuous bright light all the time. Label the line X.

(MEG GCSE Specimen paper)

Figure 2

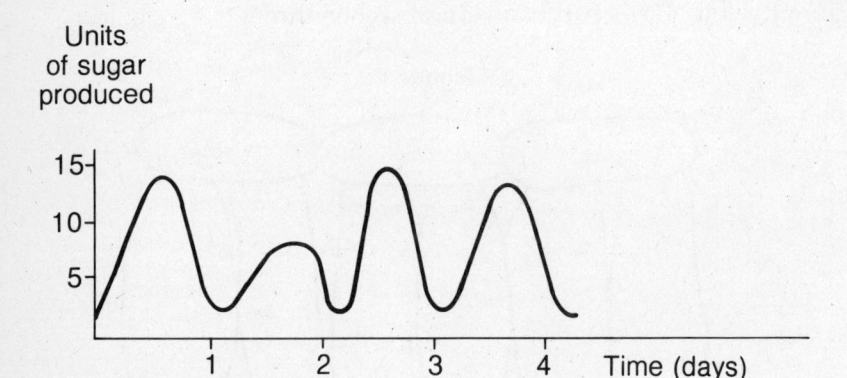

Answer
To answer parts (a) and (b) you need only to remember facts which you have been given in class. To answer part (c) you have to be able to read the graph, this means work out what it represents. Then you must relate this information to your own knowledge to come up with a reason for *why* less sugar was produced on the second day. You also have to decide where to draw the line X; to do this you will first have to work out the effect of continuous bright light using your own knowledge of photosynthesis. Then you have to represent this effect by drawing a line on the graph.

Question
Equal amounts of a dry sandy soil and a dry clay soil were placed separately in each of two boiling tubes. The two boiling tubes were placed in a beaker of cold water, which was heated for a period of 8 minutes and then allowed to cool. A thermometer was placed in each soil sample so that the temperature of both the sandy soil and the clay soil could be taken at 2-minute intervals during the heating and cooling period.

Results

	time (min)	temperature of sandy soil (°C)	temperature of clay soil (°C)
heating	0	11	11
	2	16	13
	4	22	17
	6	29	21
	8	36	26
cooling	10	35	35
	12	30	23
	14	24	21
	16	20	19

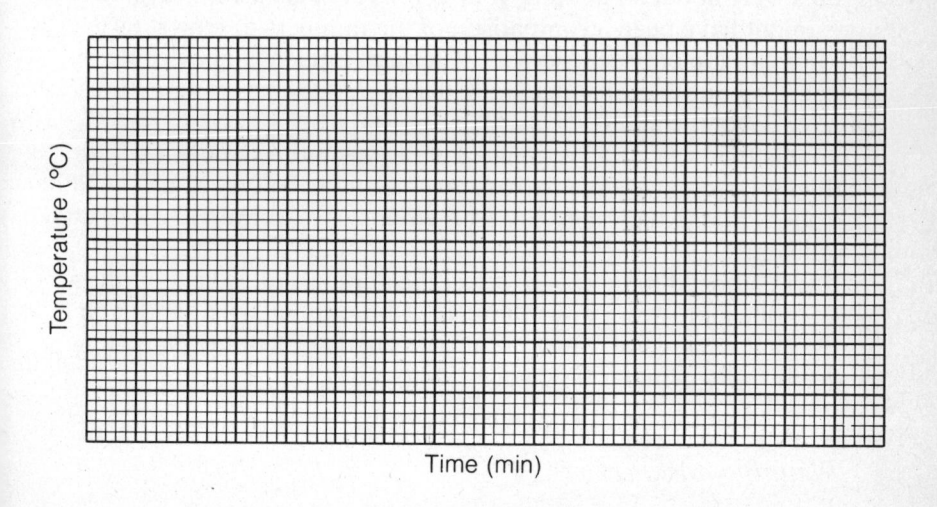

Temperature (°C)

Time (min)

a Using the axes provided, construct two curves, one to show how sandy soil heats up and cools and one to show how clay soil heats up and cools. Label your curves.

b Describe why the heating and cooling curves of the two soils are different.

c (i) Explain how the addition of lime to a heavy clay soil would improve its fertility.

(ii) State one environmental disadvantage of adding too much artificial fertiliser to sandy soil.
(iii) State one way in which the productivity of a field can be increased without destroying its soil structure.

(MEG GCSE Specimen paper)

Answer
In this question in part (a), *you* have to *draw* the graph using the table of results you have been given. In part (b), you are asked to describe *why* the results show the pattern you have drawn. You will need to make sense of these results by using your knowledge of soils. You will also need to study very carefully both your graph and the table of results. It is unlikely that you will have seen results exactly like these before, or drawn a graph like this before. So, to solve this new problem, you will have to use the skills and experience you have gained from working out similar problems.

Look back to page 23. Suppose, instead of foxglove flowers, the two sets of figures were about something you had never come across before. The figures might have been a comparison of the numbers of crows' nests found in a sample of beech trees in Wales and England. They could even have been the number of spots on the faces of Martians living on the surface or deep in craters!

The point is that you could organise the results in the same way even though you have never come across these subjects before. You now know how to *apply* mathematical skills and methods of reasoning to completely new problems.

In part (c) you need to be able to select the appropriate facts to fit these particular questions from everything you know about soils. Once you have decided what is relevant you must write down your explanations and ideas clearly using as few words as possible.

- *Planning a Project*

Doing a project can be really exciting and rewarding, but it takes a lot of hard work. It also needs careful planning if the end result is going to do justice to all your effort.

Choosing a suitable topic

This is one of the most difficult parts! It has to be a topic you are interested enough in to motivate you to keep working at the project! It should be something that will be relatively easy to find out about. Do not choose a project that is just *descriptive*. Biology is not only a descriptive science but also a *practical* science. A good project will involve actually getting some **new results** or information of some kind that you can evaluate.

The planning stage

List all your ideas about the topic and discuss with your teacher ones which are worth pursuing. Don't be too ambitious, set up realistic targets and programmes of project work so that you do not get put off halfway through.
Then **draw up a timetable** or 'plan of action' for all the jobs that you think will need to be done to complete the project. Make sure you have enough time to do them. Talk this over with your teacher and, if your plans are approved, then you are ready to start work.

What makes a good project?

Your project needs to include some of all of the following:

1 **Some background research (setting the scene).** This might involve reading textbooks, taking bits of notes from your own exercise books, taking information from library books, magazines, newspapers etc. Make sure you must know how to use the index in the book to locate the bit you need. It could involve interviewing people and noting down their views.

2 **Collecting new information on the subject yourself.** This will be the part where you go out, measure things, grow plants, keep a record of animal behaviour, monitor pollution in a particular situation or whatever. You must describe **how** and **why** you set about your field work or experimental work. You may end up with lots of notes and figures – keep a careful note of these as you go along.

3 **Organising your results and information.** This will involve processing your results into a form that is easy to understand – often using methods outlined on page 23. Any relevant information you find in your research should be included. It will be up to you to choose the best ways of presenting the new results and information.

4 **Drawing a conclusion.** Use this to summarise what you have discovered. How does your own bit of research fit in with what is known about the subject already? You may find that not all of the information you have gathered turns out to be of any use and so you will have to be careful to select the appropriate bits.

● Memorising and understanding things

One of the most difficult parts of your biology course will be to remember what you are being taught. It is always easier to remember something if you understand it and can link it up to other parts of the biology course. Try using the following suggestions:

1. Never try to memorise something that you do not understand.
2. Always try to link new materials with facts you have learnt previously.
3. Look for similarities between the new topic and other things in biology that you do understand.
4. Select the important bits and try and fix these in your mind.
5. Reorganise the new material you have been given in a way which helps you to remember it. For example,
   - underline different sections in certain colours
   - add an extra diagram or comment if it helps to make something more easy to understand
   - write down a relevant bit of theory at the beginning of an account of an experiment
   - finish off something that you got behind on in the lesson *while it is fresh in your mind*
6. Later in the day try to read through new notes you have made. Go over them *at least once* before the next lesson and check through the five points above when you do so.

● How to make a good summary

1. Include all the main ideas that appeared in the original piece.
2. Do **not** introduce any new ideas
3. Write it **in your own words**
4. Make it **well organised**, logical and easy to read.

Making summaries are a good way of sorting out the essential details about a subject. It also improves your skill in telling the difference between the main points and the less important items. When you come to make a summary, read through the main text or class notes and make a very brief note of what you think are the important bits. Underlining the main points is a good way to make a summary from your class notes. Link these main ideas together in your own words to make a summary.

Here is an example:

Main text: **What can go wrong with the circulation?**
One of the most common defects of the circulation is high blood pressure. We all develop a high blood pressure at one time or another, when we take exercise for example, but some people have high blood pressure all the time. This puts an extra strain on the heart, and may lead to heart failure. It also pushes out the walls of the arteries, and may burst them – just as a balloon will burst if you blow it up too much. The risk of this happening is greatest in old people whose arteries have become fragile. Sometimes an artery bursts inside the brain, and the spillage of blood kills the cells in that part of the brain. This results in a stroke, and it may leave the person partly paralysed and unable to speak properly. A severe stroke can be fatal.
What causes high blood pressure? We don't know, but it is frequently associated with the stress and tensions of modern life and with eating and drinking too much.
Summary:
A common defect of the circulation is high blood pressure. Some people develop permanent high blood pressure which may lead to heart failure or cause an artery to burst. If the artery bursts inside the brain, it results in a stroke.
The causes of high blood pressure are unknown, but it is often linked with stress and overeating or excessive drinking.

● *Working with Mathematics in biology*

If you look closely at the syllabus you are following in your school, you will probably be surprised at the number of skills that you are expected to acquire that involve mathematics. You might have thought that biology was not a very 'mathematical' subject, but you would be quite wrong to think this! As you will have seen from reading this book, mathematics is an important part of biology. It is invaluable in illustrating many biological concepts, presenting results and solving problems. You will find a checklist of mathematical skills on page 41, which includes all the mathematical techniques explained in this book.

● Checklist of skills for GCSE

Look at this list to remind yourself of the type of skills you should be developing as you work through your biology course.

Practical biology

1. **Doing investigations**
   Follow instructions you have been given without further advice
   Work safely – handle materials and equipment carefully
   Make accurate observations
   Make accurate measurements

2. **Recording your results accurately**
   Doing biological drawings
   Filling in tables
   Drawing graphs

3. **Interpreting results**
   Sort out important information from tables and charts.
   Sort out important information from graphs
   Recognise patterns in the results
   Do simple calculations necessary to work out what your results mean
   Draw conclusions from the results

4. **Designing your own investigations**
   Make hypotheses
   Plan and carry out investigations to test your hypotheses
   Comment on the design of an investigation. (Does it work well? Could it be improved? If so, how?)

Theoretical biology

Take notes
Cope with new words
Plan your written work
Memorise facts
Produce a good project
Write summaries
Use biological knowledge to solve problems of a theoretical kind
Apply knowledge you have learned to solve a problem about something new to you
Select and organise information about an idea
Communicate information and ideas in writing
Present reasoned explanations for biological facts and patterns
Apply biological knowledge to technical social and economic problems

Mathematical skills

Work out simple arithmetical problems
Calculate the range, the mean, the mode and the median
Construct a frequency table
Construct a grouped frequency table
Construct a bar chart
Construct a bistogram
Construct a line graph
Calculate percentages
Calculate percentage increase
Estimate results
Estimate values from line graphs
Work with fractions
Work with decimals
Complete calculations on tables of results
Understand ideas presented as graphs or tables of results

Units of measurement

Each time you measure something you should use standard units of measurement. Here are some of the most common units you will meet.

Property	Standard unit	Symbol	Useful examples
Length	**metre**	m	
	Other units:		
	centimetre ($\frac{1}{100}$ of a metre)	cm	100 cm = 1 m
	millimetre ($\frac{1}{1000}$ of a metre)	mm	10 mm = 1 cm
	micrometre ($\frac{1}{1\,000\,000}$ of a metre)	μm	1000 μm = 1 mm
Area	**square metre**	m^2	
	Other unit:		
	square centimetre	cm^2	10 000 cm^2 = 1 m^2
Volume	**cubic metre**	m^3	
	Other units:		
	cubic decimetre (litre)	dm^3	1000 dm^3 = 1 m^3
	cubic centimetre	cm^3	1000 cm^3 = 1 dm^3
Mass	**kilogramme**	kg	
	Other unit:		
	gram	g	1000 g = 1 kg
Time	**second**	s	1 minute = 60 s
Temperature	**degrees celsuis** (centigrade)	°C	100°C water boils
			0°C water freezes
Energy	**joule**	J	
	Other unit:		
	kilojoule	kJ	1000 J = 1 kJ
Force	**newton**	N	
Angle	**degrees** (*of a circle*)	°	360° in a circle

Index

answering questions *31*
   structured questions *33–36*
array *24*
averages *20–21*
   mean *20, 27*
   median *20, 27*
   mode *21, 27*
   range *20, 27*
axes *13*

bar chart *17*
biological drawings *10*
biological words *31, 32*

calculations
   averages *20–21*
   error *19*
   percentages *12, 21*
   error *19*
   percentages *12, 21*
   percentages error *19*
   percentage increase *21–22*
conclusions *27–28*
controls *6–7*
cross-references *28*

data *2*
drawings, biological *10*

errors *18–19*
   calculation *19*
   percentage error *19*

fitting a line *14*
frequency tables *16, 23*
   grouped *24, 25, 26*

graphs *12–15*
   axes *13*
   estimating values *14, 15*
   fitting a line *14*
   origin *13*
   scales *14*

histograms *16–17, 25, 26*
hypothesis *2*

investigations *2–3*
   planning *7*
   report writing *9*

mean *20, 27*
median *20, 27*
memorising things *38*
mode *20, 27*

notes *30–31*

observations
   qualitative *2*
   quantitative *2*
origin (graphs) *13*

percentages *12, 21*
   calculation *21*
   percentage error *19*
   percentage increase *21–22*
planning answers *31*
   investigations *7*
   projects *37*

projects
  choosing at topic *36*
  planning *37*
  research *37*

range *20, 27*
report writing *9*
research *37*
results *8*

scales
  drawings *10*
  graphs *14*
scientific method *2–3*
standard (SI) units *41*
summary writing *38–39*
structured questions *33–36*

tables *11*
  frequency tables *16, 23*
  grouped frequency tables *24*

units *41*

variables *5–6*

writing reports *9*
writing up results *8*